THE WALKS

C000263601

WALK 1 page 7. *Bathampton Toll Bridge, the Kennet & A...*
Grade 1. 3.0 kms/2 miles. Approximate time 1 hour. Total ascent:

WALK 2 page 10. *The George via Kennet and Avon can...*
Hampton Wharf Swing Bridge, Holcombe Farm Lane and
Grade 1. 2.4 kms/1.5 miles. Approximate time 40 minutes. Total ascent: 41 metres.

WALK 3 page 12. *Bathampton Down and Sham Castle.*
Grade 2. 3.7 kms/2.3 miles. Approximate time 1 hour 20 minutes. Total ascent: 158 metres.

WALK 4 page 15. *Over the Downs to Claverton.*
Grade 2. 9 kms/5.6 miles. Approximate time 2 hours 45 minutes. Total ascent: 190 metres.

WALK 5 page 19. *Around Bathampton and Claverton Downs.*
Grade 2. 8.5 kms/5.3 miles (or with extension, Grade 3. 12.2 kms/7.6 miles).
Approximate time - Main Route: 2 hours 45 minutes, with extension 4 hours. Total ascent: 175/215 metres.

WALK 6 page 23. *Bathampton to Smallcombe, Rainbow Wood, Widcombe*
and the Kennet & Avon Canal.
Grade 3. 9.75 kms/6 miles. Approximate time 3 hours. Total ascent: 340 metres.

WALK 7 page 27. *Brown's Folly, Dundas Aqueduct and the Kennet & Avon Canal.*
Grade 2/3. 12.5 kms/8 miles. Approximate time 4 hours. Total ascent: 255 metres.

WALK 8 page 30. *Bathford, Kingsdown, Monkton Farleigh and Brown's Folly.*
Grade 2. 9.8 kms/6.1 miles. Approximate time 3 hours. Total ascent: 220 metres.

WALK 9 page 33. *Batheaston to St Catherine's Court.*
Grade 2. 8.8kms/5.5 miles. Approximate time 3 hours. Total ascent: 276 metres.

WALK 10 page 36. *Batheaston to Bathford, Shockerwick and Bannerdown.*
Grade 2/3. 8 kms/5 miles or 10.4 kms/6.5 miles from Bathampton.
Approximate time 2 hours 40 minutes or from Bathampton 3 hours 10 minutes. Total ascent: 200 metres.

WALK 11 page 38. *Three Hills Walk.*
Grade 3. 12 kms/7.5 miles. Approximate time 4 hours 20 minutes. Total ascent 450 metres.

WALK 12 page 41. *Four Churches Walk.*
Main walk Grade 3. 11.3 kms/7 miles. Shorter version Grade 2. 7.4 kms/4.7 miles. Add 3.2 kms/2 miles for Bathampton start.
Approximate time: Main route 3 hours 45 mins. Shorter route 2 hours 30 minutes. (+1hour for Bathampton start)
Total ascent: Main route 350 metres; Shorter route 180 metres.

Note: Abbreviation occurring in text throughout this book. **PF = Public Footpath; 00' = Minutes**

Please follow the Country Code!

- Enjoy the countryside - respect its life and work
- Guard against all risk of fire
- Fasten all gates
- Keep dogs under close control, especially amongst sheep
- Leave livestock, crops and machinery alone
- Use gates and stiles to cross fences, hedges or walls

- Take your litter home
- Help to keep all water clean
- Protect wildlife, plants and trees
- Take special care on country roads
- Make no unnecessary noise
- Keep to designated public rights of way

Walks around Bathampton

INTRODUCTION

The Bathampton Footpaths Association, formerly known as the Bathampton Downs Public Paths Association, was founded nearly 25 years ago to safeguard public rights of way across Bathampton Down which were endangered by the application to divert some of the public footpaths across the golf course without adequate consultation with the local community.

Thanks to the hard work of the Association's officers, these rights were preserved.

Now the challenge is to involve a new generation of walkers, from within our community and from further afield, in using these rights of way, not only on Bathampton Down, but also on the Downs and valleys around us. Only by people walking them will they be kept open. If that does not happen they will become overgrown with brambles and briars, nettles and long grass.

We have published this book in the hope that it will help to ensure the survival of our ancient public footpaths. The publication has been made possible by the generous assistance of the trustees of the Miller Trust, established in the Will of former residents of Bathampton to improve the lives of those who live in the village. We are also grateful to the Bathampton Parish Council for a generous grant.

Several of the route descriptions have been written by Gill Huggins, for many years the Association's Secretary and Walks Co-ordinator and by Prabir Nandi our former Chairman. Others have been written by myself with help from two of our members, Betty Hayward and Marc Plenty. Prabir has also taken all the photographs without which this would be a dull thing indeed.

My thanks also go to the Association members and others who acted as guinea pigs and tried out the walks using our notes and maps. Their comments have been useful in correcting mistakes and avoiding ambiguities. They and other friends have also helped with proof reading.

Stuart Burroughs, Curator of the Bath at Work Museum, accepted my invitation to write the Foreword within a ridiculously short time and carried it out brilliantly.

Finally, my thanks go to Richard Maby who has designed this book and created a gem from unsophisticated material.

F O R W A R D !

by Stuart Burroughs

If you stand, to catch your breath after the steep climb, on the northern escarpment edge of Bathampton Down and let your eyes drift across the prospect from west to east, you see laid out a landscape shaped by the elements and man in equal measure. This is a landscape where the counties of Wiltshire, Somerset and Gloucestershire meet and where the serried ranks of Georgian terraces and the clamour of tourist traffic of the city of Bath meet the rolling hillsides of the countryside which surround it.

Gazing across the valley of the River Avon you will see rising before you the southernmost extension of the Cotswolds - Lansdown, Charmy Down, Solsbury Hill and Bannerdown, the most visible local evidence of the great limestone ridge which straddles England from the Humber to the Dorset Coast.

The limestone capping, through which the River Avon and its tributary brooks have made their way, provided the Bath stone for that city's famous architecture. In Medieval times, Bath was equally well known for the quality of its woollen cloth made from the fine wool of the sheep which thrived on the surrounding well-drained downs.

The River Avon here is nearing the end of its journey to the Bristol Channel and after cutting a northerly route through the Limpley Stoke valley to the east, turns sharply west as it comes into sight of Bath. The Avon and its tributaries which have cut through the limestone ridge have exposed the clay beneath, helping to weather the landscape into soft rounded downs and valleys. The Lam Brook and St Catherine's Brook have carved the valleys which have isolated Solsbury Hill. Further to the east the By Brook has cut through the great valley heading east to Shockerwick and Box. Along all these brooks, man has taken advantage of the swiftly flowing water, building watermills along their length. Within Batheaston, on St Catherine's Brook, stood a watermill which at its start was used to grind corn, then became a cloth mill and finally in 1827 became a mill for throwing silk - i.e. for twisting several threads of silk together to make a stronger one.

Bathampton and Bathampton Down

There has been human habitation here since ancient times. On Bathampton Down itself (Walk 3) there is evidence of use as far back as the Bronze Age and although the round barrows from this period have been lost, an enclosure, now largely covered by a golf course, may date from the Iron Age although adapted in more recent times. At one time the post-Roman Wansdyke was thought to have crossed the down but this is now thought unlikely. A system of Iron Age field boundaries, most clearly visible running at right angles across several of the golf course fairways as a series of almost parallel ridges, can be seen on the slopes down to Bathampton. From at least the 18th century, Bath Stone (a form of limestone) was quarried and mined here and in 1808 a steeply inclined tramway (featured in Walk 4) conveyed stone in wagons from the quarries to the Kennet & Avon Canal hundreds of feet below.

Bathampton village is the point where most of these walks start and finish and a brief description of this settlement is in order. – *hampton* is a place name which may derive from its place as a principal village or farmstead of an area *(ham tun)*. Certainly there was settlement here in the 11th century and a vicarage by the 14th. Agriculture thrived on the well-watered meadows and the well-drained downlands. In the 19th century the village was divided by the construction of the Kennet & Avon Canal and the Great Western Railway but continued to grow. The church, dedicated to St. Nicholas, contains a memorial to Admiral Arthur Phillip, the first governor of New South Wales. Phillip was buried in the church in 1814 and although it was unnoticed for many years, the grave was discovered in 1897 and the Premier of New South Wales, Sir Henry Parkes, had it restored. The Australia Chapel, in the south aisle, commemorates Phillip and was constructed in 1974 using Australian materials in its floors and furnishings.

Limpley Stoke Valley and its Canals

In the south east, in the Limpley Stoke valley, villages cling to the hillside in what, historically, has been an unstable geological area characterised by landslips in the rough clay. Against the western side, the A36 Warminster Road (a 19th century turnpike road) and the Kennet & Avon Canal hug the hillside almost challenging the geology to do its worst. Below them are the River Avon itself and the railway line to Weymouth.

The **Kennet & Avon Canal** was proposed in 1788 and completed as far as Bathampton by 1810, linking with the **Somerset Coal Canal** near Limpley Stoke at the Dundas Aqueduct. Constructed to supply Bath and Bristol with coal from North Somerset, the Somerset Coal Canal (see Walk 5) closed in the 1890s although a short stretch of it can be seen near the village of Monkton Combe at the Dundas basin. The K & A ceased to be used for commercial traffic after 1951 but was saved from becoming totally derelict by sporadic preservation work by volunteers. Systematic restoration commenced in the mid-1960s and by the end of the century the canal was navigable from Reading at its eastern end to Bath at its western. (Walks 1, 2. 4, 6 and 7 include sections of the canal.)

Claverton village (Walk 4) is set facing Warleigh where the Avon valley is at its most beautiful. To the north of the village church is the site of an Elizabethan manor house whose garden terraces and gates remain. In 1820 Claverton Manor was rebuilt much higher up the hillside and is now home to the American Museum in Britain. Above the manor, on Claverton Down, is the University of Bath which gained its charter in 1966. In the churchyard is buried the famous 18th century postal pioneer and stone-mine owner Ralph Allen, who died in 1764. His tomb rests under a pyramid raised on arcades in modest Roman splendour.

Below the village is the former watermill converted in the early 1800s to pump water from the River Avon to top up the Kennet & Avon Canal.

Brown's Folly or 'The Pepperpot' peeps above the tree line on the eastern slopes of the Avon Valley

Bathford and its Neighbours

Across the valley are the heights of **Kingsdown** and **Monkton Farleigh** (Walk 8) where there were formerly Bath stone mines, and the well wooded slopes of Bathford Hill below **Brown's Folly** (Walks 7 & 8) that obscure the jagged rock faces of old stone-mining activity. The Folly is a belvedere tower built in 1840 by a local landowner, Charles Wade Brown. Even with the trees in full leaf this austere tower is an unmistakable landmark.

Below the hilltop is the steeply arranged and attractive village of **Bathford** (Walks 7, 8 &10) which covers an area stretching from Shockerwick to the north to Warleigh in the south. With Roman villas at both Warleigh and Horselands below the village, this is a settlement with ancient roots. Since at least 940 (when reference is made to 'the place called Forde') this village, on two river fords, and on an historically important road junction, has flourished as an agricultural centre. A watermill on the By Brook, which joins the Avon here, may be the oldest continuously operated industrial site in the area. At present the mill is engaged in making speciality papers.

Georgian splendour at Shockerwick House

Shockerwick House (Walk 10) is a manor house on the edge of the village now run as a residential home. It was once thought to have been designed by the famous architect John Wood, although this now seems to be in doubt. Prime Minister William Pitt The Younger visited the house in 1805 and Queen Victoria visited in 1830 when, as Princess Victoria, she officially opened Bath's Royal Victoria Park.

Batheaston and the Southern Cotswolds

The A4 London Road enters the Avon valley from the east and passing through **Batheaston** village follows the route of the Roman Fosse Way into Bath. The Fosse Way was a Roman military road built in the first century AD. From Batheaston it slopes north east over Bannerdown and a long straight stretch of it can be seen on Walk 10.

Immediately north of Batheaston is the boundary with Gloucestershire and the parish shares its eastern edge with the county of Wiltshire. In the northern hinterland of the village the land rises to over 600 feet at Solsbury Hill, Charmy Down and Bannerdown (Walk 11) and stone from these southernmost tips of the Cotswolds is evident in the buildings of the village. Dating from at least as early as the 10th century the village has flourished. It has regained something of its village nature with the completion of a major road bypass in the mid-1990s.

Up the St Catherine's Brook behind Batheaston are two large storage reservoirs built in the late 19th century. At Monkswood, where the earliest one was built in the 1870s, a hoard of Bronze age valuables was found during construction.

Solsbury Hill, which falls within the parish of Batheaston, is one of the most easily identified landscape features in the area. Rising to 625 feet this smoothly rounded hill gives spectacular views of the city from its summit. On the hilltop are the clearly discernible remains of an Iron Age hill fort. Occupied from around 300 BC to 100 BC, this fort was surrounded by a 4 metre high rampart faced with dry stone walls both inside and out. The fort was abandoned before the Roman invasion of the first century AD.

Behind Solsbury Hill is Charmy Down where the remains of an airfield built in the Second World War can be seen.

Villages of the Upper Swainswick Valley

Below the hill and in the valley of the Lam Brook are the villages of **Swainswick** and **Woolley** (Walk 12). Swainswick, another medieval village, is the place where the mythical King Bladud first noticed that the pigs he had been forced to tend after he contracted leprosy, wallowed in the hot spring waters and were cured of their disease. Following their example Bladud himself was miraculously cured of this disfiguring disease.

The famous architects John Wood the Elder and the Younger who were responsible for the design of many of Bath's most famous Georgian features, are buried in Swainswick church.

Woolley, on the Lam Brook, is one of the 'Thankful Villages', from which no resident of eligible age was killed during the First World War. Of the thirteen men who served in the 1914-18 war from the village, two were injured but none died. The church is by John Wood the Younger and the watermill was used during the 18th century in the making of gunpowder. In this, as in most 'powder mills', the roofs and floors were not firmly fixed so that in the case of an explosion they would be blown off whilst the less easily repaired walls would be preserved!

On the heights of Bathampton Down (Walk 3), where even on the hottest of days there is a cool breeze, this landscape is laid out like a scale model. These walks invite you to explore an area within easy reach of Bath and, if you think you know the city's history, prepare to see part of the rural hinterland that has traditionally sustained it.

The city of Bath seen from above Bathf... a panorama typical of many to be had fr... vantage points along the walks in this bo...

Starting Point:
- Unmetalled section of The George car park
Grid Ref: OS776:665 Explorer Map 155
Distance: 3 kms/2 miles
Approximate time: 1 hour
Total Ascent: 42 metres

Summary:
This is an easy walk in and around Bathampton. Some of the most interesting buildings in the village will be seen, and there is also a walk across the Meadows.

✳ = See 'Points of Note' at the end of this walk.

Let's Go!

● Leaving The George✳ car park turn left and walk along Mill Lane. Just before the railway bridge, on the right hand side of the road, you will see the rusty remnants of a gate. This led onto the footpath for passengers using Bathampton Station until its closure in 1966. The station was situated about 200 metres east of the bridge.

The George and Kennet & Avon Canal

Continue along the lane past a PF stile in the hedge on your left. Pass the entrance to Bathampton Manor.✳ Shortly you will arrive at the Toll Bridge which looks old but was built in the nineteenth century.

The river is the Avon which rises near Malmesbury and flows all the way to Bristol and thence into the Bristol Channel.

The buildings on each side of the bridge were formerly mills✳. The one on the north side still retains a millwheel, a replica of the original one. On the wall of the toll house is a list of the charges from a century ago. This is one of very few operating toll bridges still in existence in Britain.

The weir downstream of the bridge was built to divert water to operate the mill wheel of the mills on both sides of the river.

● From the Toll Bridge retrace your steps along Mill Lane for some 250 metres. Cross the stile in the hedge on your right. From here the route goes across the meadows. The path is quite clear and veers gradually towards the far right hand corner of the first pasture. It comes to a wooden bridge with a stile on each end. Cross the bridge and the stiles. Ignore the track to your left. Cross the next field with the field edge on your left and gradually veer right under the electricity pylons. On your left are some rundown farm buildings. Passing the farm buildings to your left, aim for the left-hand arch of the bypass bridge. Join a track as you go under the bridge and leave it again when you emerge at the other side through a gate. Head across the grassy meadow with the pylons to your right. Shortly you will reach a bridge over a ditch. Cross the bridge and follow the hedge on your left uphill to the corner of the field and through a kissing gate. Continue up a track and shortly turn right on to Meadow Lane.

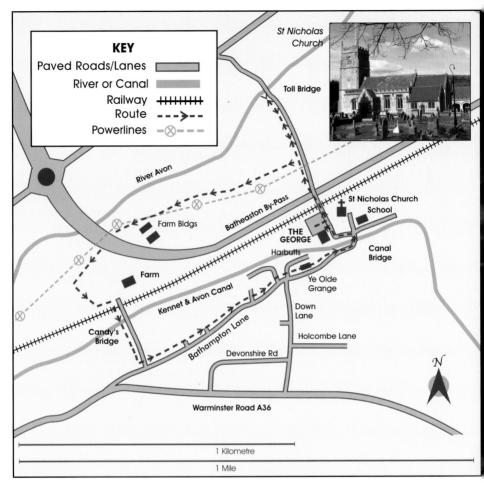

KEY

Paved Roads/Lanes
River or Canal
Railway
Route
Powerlines

St Nicholas Church

Toll Bridge

River Avon

Batheaston By-Pass

Farm Bldgs

St Nicholas Church School

THE GEORGE

Harbutts

Canal Bridge

Farm

Kennet & Avon Canal

Ye Olde Grange

Down Lane

Candy's Bridge

Bathampton Lane

Holcombe Lane

Devonshire Rd

N

Warminster Road A36

1 Kilometre

1 Mile

Cross the railway and the canal bridge, known locally as Candy's Bridge. Carry on up to the top of Meadow Lane (40').

● At the top of Meadow Lane the large house on the left has a false window. Can you spot it? This is a feature of houses built between the 17th and early 19th centuries when a 'window tax' was levied on all houses having more than a certain number of windows. This induced some thrifty householders to paint windows on their houses to keep up appearances! This tax was abolished in 1851 in favour of a property tax similar to the local council tax of the present day.

● On Bathampton Lane, turn left and go down the Lane, past some imposing Georgian houses, then three modern houses, until you arrive at Glebe Cottage. Just over the garden wall of Glebe Cottage is a very old stone arch, the remains of a former priory.

● Walk on past Down Lane and Kennet Park until you arrive at The Harbutts. There was once a farmyard here, next to Harbutts Plasticine factory. At the entrance to 'The Harbutts' a plaque commemorates the site of the Plasticine factory which closed in 1983.

About 30 metres down the street, on the gable wall of 'Ye Grange', is a bust of William Harbutt

who lived here. He was the inventor of Plasticine and founder of the factory. Built in 1661, this is one of the oldest houses in the village. The ancient wisteria growing over its front wall produces luxuriant blooms in early summer.

Across the street from 'Ye Grange' is the Dog's Head Trough, a rectangular stone trough into which spring water flows the whole year round. Before mains supply arrived, this was the primary source of water for the village.

Further on there is a row of old cottages, the largest of which, with a post box in the wall, was until recently the village shop and post office. A few yards on, the first house of Chapel Row used to be a newspaper and sweet shop. Look closely, their old doorways have been closed up and their doors are now on the other side of the cottages.

Crossing the canal bridge near the end of this walk, St Nicholas Church* is straight in front of you. The Primary School is to your right and The George to your left. The Church and churchyard are well worth a visit (20').

Ye Grange, built 1661.

POINTS OF NOTE

The George
It is said that The George dates from the 12th century and was originally part of a monastery under the Prior of Bath. Since the Reformation nearly 500 years ago it has been an inn for travellers and more recently a pub .

River Avon Toll Bridge Mills
In the 1950s the southernmost mill was a tea room and the low building nearest to the car park provided changing rooms for people wanting to bathe in the river in summer for which they were charged the equivalent of 3 pence!

Bathampton Manor
Ralph Allen, whose Combe Down quarries supplied the stone for building Georgian Bath, owned the manor from the mid-1700s. It remained in the Allen family until 1921 when his extensive estate around Bathampton was sold.

St Nicholas Church
There has been a church on this site for nearly 800 years. Most of the present building was built by Ralph Allen around 1750 with some later additions. Inside the church is the resting place of Admiral Arthur Phillip, the founder of New South Wales. The Australia Chapel was opened in 1974 and is dedicated to his memory. There are also memorials to other important historical figures.

The oldest artifact is the stone figure in the external wall of the church near the vestry door.

In the churchyard are the graves of the famous artist, Walter Sickert who owned St George's House on Bathampton Lane and Viscount Jean Baptiste du Barry who was killed in a duel on Bathampton Down. William Harbutt is buried here as is Elsie Luke, murdered in 1891 on Bathampton Down. Her murder remains unsolved.

Starting Point:

- Unmetalled section of The George car park

Grid Ref: OS776:665 Explorer Map 155

Distance: 2.4 kms/ 1.5 miles

Approximate time:

40/50 minutes (main/alternative route)

Total Ascent: 41 metres

Summary:

A beautiful circular walk along the towpath to the wooden swing bridge at Hampton Wharf. Up a short grassy slope and back through the village to The George. There are lovely views from the towpath and the slope above Hampton Wharf.

✳ = See 'Points of Interest' at the end of this walk.

Let's Go!

● Turn right out of the car park and go up the steps in front of the pub onto the Kennet and Avon Canal✳ towpath. Turn left (east) and head towards the bridge, No.183, that carries the road from Bathampton to the Toll Bridge. Note the grooves on the edge of the wall about waist height made by the ropes attached to the horses which were pulling the barges. Note also the masons' marks and some early dates carved into the stone blocks underneath the arch, for example, *IL 1808* and *AL 1843*. Bridges are numbered from the Reading end of the canal.

● Carry on past the playing fields on your right. The second of the three houses on the left is Canal Farm House, belonging to one of the former five working farms in Bathampton Parish. At the next bend some 200 yards further on, you will see that the canal widens. This is a winding hole where boats could turn. One more bend and you will see ahead of you Hampton Wharf✳ with its cottage and swing bridge (20').

● Cross the bridge* and go through the kissing gate to the left of the private gate. Pass through and ascend the path uphill with a hawthorn hedge on your right.

*(Alternative Route starts here.)

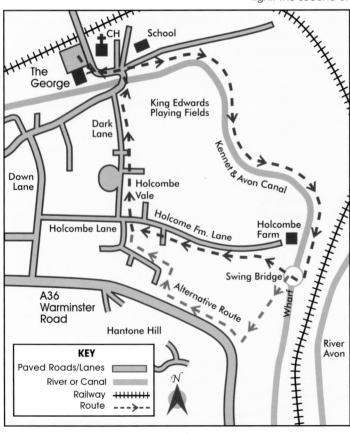

Follow the path until you come to a kissing gate. where you enter Holcombe Farm Lane which takes you to the centre of Bathampton (10'). Opposite the village shops turn right into Holcombe Vale and follow it to the bottom. Straight ahead take a footpath between two garden fences into Dark Lane at the foot of which you reach Bathampton High Street where you turn right, over the canal bridge, and then left to the George (10').

*Alternative Route

Instead of taking the path to Holcombe Farm Lane, cross the swing bridge and turn left along the wharf. At its end, cross a ditch, go over a stile and climb the path which follows the lower end of the old tramway from the quarries on Bathampton Down. At the top, go over a stile, descend to the A36 and turn right along the pavement for 200m until opposite a PF sign on the other side of the road. Turn right, go down some steps onto a paved path and thence to a road. Continue along it until the first turning to the right which brings you out at the village shops where you rejoin the main route (20').

POINTS OF NOTE

The Kennet and Avon Canal

The canal was built between 1794 and 1810. It was designed by the famous Scottish engineer John Rennie who also designed London Bridge. This canal represented a great boon to the transport of heavy goods between Bristol and London; previously they would have gone by sea around the western and southern coasts of England. Eventually canals were almost put out of business by the railways although a small amount of commercial traffic continued on this canal until 1951.

Thereafter, the canal was neglected and became un-navigable until it was restored in the 1980s and was reopened by the Queen in 1990 on the restoration of the Caen Hill flight of locks near Devizes.

Hampton Wharf swing bridge

This is where a wooden bridge can be swung open to permit boats to pass through. It is also the site of a wharf where stone from the quarries on Bathampton Down was loaded onto barges (see Walk No 4).

The swing bridge and cottage at Hampton Wharf

Parking: Devonshire Road off Down Lane.

Start: From the Scout Hall opposite the top of Down Lane on the A36.

Grid Ref: (Parking) OS776:659
(Start OS776:658)
Explorer Map 155

Distance: 3.7 kms/2.3 miles

Approximate time: 1 hour 20 minutes

Total Ascent: 158 metres

Summary:

One fairly steep ascent and descent, otherwise mostly flat grassy terrain. Parts can be muddy in winter. An opportunity to see ancient field systems and outstanding views of the Avon and Box valleys and over the City of Bath.

✳ = See 'Points of Interest' at the end of this walk.

Let's Go!

● Head up the track marked by the bridleway sign which is a few metres in from the main road.

This is a very ancient route worn down over the centuries by the passage of men, packhorses and mules and livestock bound for market.

● Go through a metal gate with a notice stating that from here the land belongs to Bath Golf Club (6').

The land was purchased from the Ralph Allen estate when it was sold in various lots in 1921. Less than half this land is occupied by the golf course, the rest consists of woodland and rough pasture.

The track bends left then right between high banks and can often be wet at this point. On reaching the woods ignore a stile on your left with a sign indicating you are crossing the Bath Skyline Walk (8').

30 yards above this point was the start of a tramway built about 300 years ago that took

Bath stone from mines, now hidden in the nearby woods on your left, to the stone masons' yards close to the River Avon at Bathwick.

● The path soon bears sharply to the left (southwards) up a grassy slope to a wooden gate in the golf course boundary fence (5').

From many points there are outstanding views across the Avon valley to the Downs to the north. On these grassy slopes, in the pre-motor car age, families used to come to picnic and play.

Go through the gate and straight past a green on your left. Take care crossing in case there are golf balls flying in from the right. Continue up a short incline to the upper part of the golf course. Be aware that golfers are driving off from the tee a mere 30 metres to the left of the path. There is a sign for the bridleway that continues across the golf course and one for the footpath pointing to the right (west) which you now follow along the edge of the escarpment✳.

Walk along the escarpment for 500 metres until a wall is met. With the wall on your right the footpath turns towards the south *(14')*. *On the other side of the stone wall are deep hollows caused by the excavation of Bath stone. Beyond the nearby green a patch of woodland hides the entrance to a stone mine that was tunnelled eastwards for one kilometre more or less under where you are walking. The stone was carried by tramway to the River Avon close to the present junction of canal and river.*

(Walk 3 continues after the map)

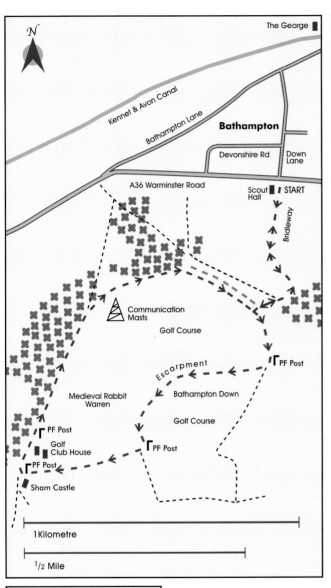

The George ▮

Kennet & Avon Canal

Bathampton Lane

Bathampton

Devonshire Rd

Down Lane

A36 Warminster Road

Scout Hall ▮ ▮ START

Bridleway

Communication Masts

Golf Course

Escarpment

PF Post

Medieval Rabbit Warren

Bathampton Down

Golf Course

PF Post

PF Post

Golf Club House

PF Post

Sham Castle

1 Kilometre

$^1/_2$ Mile

Kelston Round Hill

Freezing Hill

Distant views to be seen from Bathampton Down

Batheaston

KEY

Paved Roads/Lanes	▭
Canal	▭
Woodland	✖ ✖ ✖
Route	- - ➤ - -
Public Footpaths	- - - - -
Permissive Path	· · · · · · ·

● In a further 100 metres, before a patch of trees, is a public footpath junction. Turn to the right. Keep a sharp lookout for flying golf balls coming from the left. Cross the fairway, through a thin belt of trees and then another fairway where the direction of play is from the right. Join a track and descend towards the golf clubhouse* (6'). At the foot of the track, to the left, is Sham Castle*.

Sham Castle

● Turn right, past one car park, then along the back of the clubhouse, through another car park to a gate and a stile (3'). Climb it and follow the wide track that skirts the southern edge of the woods.

● The track peters out at the communication masts (12'). Carry straight on across the grass until you reach the edge of the woods where you will pick up a good track again. With the woods on your left you will soon reach a gateway with a metal stile at its side (3'). *2000 years ago this was the site of a Roman homestead. The outlines are still visible in aerial photographs.*

● From the gateway proceed straight ahead to an old post at about 40 metres distance. At this post veer right up a bank emerging onto an open stretch of pasture land. This is a permissive path that joins a broader path in a further 40 metres where you turn left keeping close to the escarpment. As you walk along you can enjoy wide-ranging views across the Avon valley. After about 300 metres you rejoin the bridleway about 20 metres above the Skyline Walk sign and stile on your right. Ignore them and continue down the bridleway until you reach the Scout Hall and your starting point on the A36. (22')

POINTS OF NOTE

Escarpment

The escarpment marks a geological fault line called the Hengrove Fault. There are wonderful panoramic views on this escarpment walk. The meadow on your left is covered in wild flowers in spring and is a haven for larks which nest there.

Sham Castle

This "folly" was built by Ralph Allen in 1762 to be admired from his office window in the city below. While Sham Castle is meant to be admired from below, it also provides wonderful views over Bath and of some of its famous features such as the Abbey and Camden Crescent. The northern skyline has interesting landmarks such as Kelston Round Hill with a clump of trees on its summit.

Bath Golf Club

Bath Golf Club, founded in 1880, is one of the oldest in south west England.

Ancient Farming on the Down

By looking up towards the golf fairways you will see some ridges crossing them[i]. The ridges continue across nearby pastures but are more difficult to discern because of the long grass. They mark the old Romano-British field boundaries.

In the area of rough pasture between the track and the fairways there was a rabbit warren in medieval times where rabbits were farmed for their meat and skins.

Starting Point:
- Unmetalled section of The George car park
Grid Ref: OS776:665 Explorer Map 155
Distance: 9 kms/5.6 miles
Approximate time: 2 hours 45 minutes
Total Ascent: 190 metres
Summary:

A steep ascent to the Downs and a descent via footpaths, lanes and canal towpath. The walk includes remnants of local quarrying activities and the opportunity for exploring the village of Claverton and Claverton Pumping Station.

✳ = See 'Points of Note' at the end of this walk.

Let's Go!

● From the car park turn right and join the canal towpath. Follow this left and eastwards, away from Bath and into the valley of the River Avon. The slopes of Bathampton Down can be seen to your right and to your left the tower of Bathford church and the slopes of Bathford Hill with Brown's Folly (the Pepperpot) atop it.

(The lengthman carried out maintenance on a "length" of the canal). Cross the bridge and bear left along the side of the canal. (20')

This is Hampton Wharf where boats were loaded with stone from the quarries on Bathampton Down. The stone was conveyed to the canal-side on wagons by means of a tramway using rails fixed to stone sleepers. It was then placed onto the boats using a hand propelled crane.

● At the end of the wharf cross a stile and proceed uphill.

You are now following the line of the tramway. On this path you will enjoy the beauty of the Avon Valley as it stretches south eastwards.

This view gives a good example of how the river has cut its way down through the various bands of rock over many thousands of years.

Looking to the north, the valley bottom widens as other water courses and valleys join the river, courses that once carried

It will be noted that the bend in the canal after Glen Cottage is much wider. This is a winding hole, used for the turning of barges. As the canal straightens a swing bridge comes into view with what was once a lengthman's cottage on its left-hand side.

glacial melt from the Ice Age and gave rise to the landscape we see today.

Climb a stile and follow the path to the main A36 (Bath-Warminster Road). Turn right along the pavement and follow it round the bend of

(Walk 4 continues overleaf)

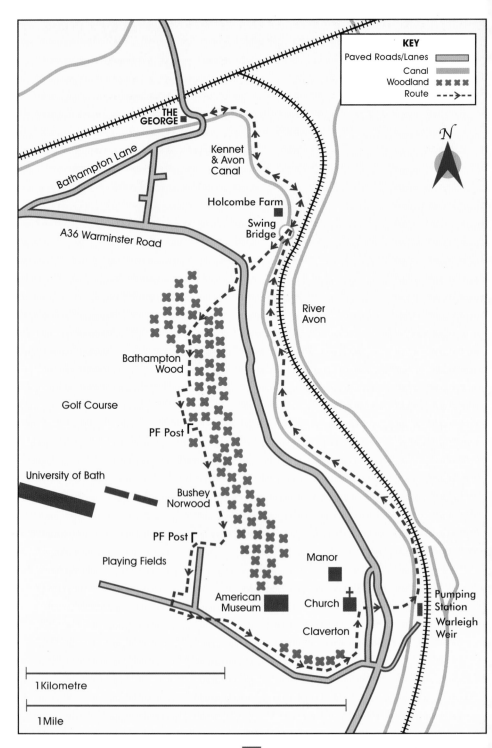

KEY
Paved Roads/Lanes
Canal
Woodland
Route

THE GEORGE

Bathampton Lane

Kennet & Avon Canal

A36 Warminster Road

Holcombe Farm

Swing Bridge

River Avon

Bathampton Wood

Golf Course

PF Post

University of Bath

Bushey Norwood

PF Post

Playing Fields

Manor

American Museum

Church

Claverton

Pumping Station

Warleigh Weir

1 Kilometre

1 Mile

the road until you are opposite the first house on your left. Here there is a PF signpost. Cross the road with care and follow the path which rejoins the tramway after 100 metres (15').

Stone sleepers mark the route of the tramway

Down to your left are the remains of a stone bridge, locally known as "Dry Arch"*. As the path climbs up the hill you can't fail to notice the lines of the stone sleepers that carried the rails, and the holes into which securing pegs were inserted.

● Keep walking in a straight line up the tramway, crossing the Bath Skyline Walk. After a last uphill scramble, the ground flattens and you emerge from the woodland virtually at the top of the hill. As the path turns left a secluded dell is on your right. This used to be one of the largest stone quarries on Bathampton Down (20').

● Having turned left you now leave the line of the tramway behind and the path rises gently to another level. Continue ahead, noticing the many gullies to your right along the way - these are all part of previous quarrying, and to your left the 'spoils' cascade down the hill side.

You will come to a stone stack covered in ivy, locally known as 'The Devil's Table' - another remnant from past quarrying. Go around the stack past a barred low cave entrance and climb a short flight of steps onto the golf course (5'). Turn left. After

St Marys Church, Claverton, with its distinctive galleon weathervane, shown left

about 200 metres, look for a path on the left to a PF post and back into woods (3'). Proceed gently downhill for 50 metres until you meet a path (Skyline Walk) at right angles. Turn right and follow this path for 50 metres through a kissing gate into Bushey Norwood (NT) (2').

● Go straight on into a large field keeping close to a fence and woodland on your left. Continue along the edge of the field until you meet a stone wall. Turn right and with the wall on your left carry on to the next corner. Cross the stone stile with a PF post next to a vehicle access gate (15').

Beyond the stile follow a well-made path. Ignore a path and gate to the left. Your path swings right and meets a track. Go left a few metres to a gate and through it to Claverton Hill Road (2'). Turn left and follow the road downhill to Claverton Village passing the gateway to Claverton Manor, now the American Museum, on your left. Take the left-hand turning into Claverton some 50 metres before the main (A36) road (15').

On turning left, the old school is immediately on your left. Continue on past attractive old houses and converted barns to St Mary's Church which is worth exploring.

Further along the lane (10'), you will see the cobbled entrance, grand gates, steps and terracing that led to the original Manor House.

● A few metres before theses gates, turn right at an open grassy space and with a stone wall on your right, take the path to the A36. Cross it with care and walk left for 50 metres, to an opening on your right leading to a gate into a field. Head downhill slightly to your right to a stone stile in the wall which leads into Ferry Lane. Go down the lane, over the canal bridge and turn left to rejoin the tow path(10'). Turn right and head back to Bathampton, the canal on your left, and return to your starting point at the George (50').

● Instead of joining the towpath you can continue to the foot of Ferry Lane and cross the railway line with care. Claverton Pumping Station* is on your left. If you bear right over the meadow you will find an excellent picnic spot next to Warleigh Weir on the

Imposing gateway at old Claverton Manor

River Avon. Warliegh Manor, until recently the home of the Skrine family, the local lords of the manor, is a short distance downstream on the other side of the river.

POINTS OF NOTE

Tramway and "Dry Arch" bridge

This sunken track is part of the original route to Claverton and when the tramway was constructed this bridge was built to carry the stone wagons over the old road. When the 'New Warminster Road' was built a further arch had to be constructed to convey the tramway over the new cutting. The tram track eventually became redundant and subsequent road widening schemes led to the second 'Dry Arch' being dismantled.

St Mary's Church, Claverton and Ralph Allen's Mausoleum

Opposite the main door of the church is the mausoleum of Ralph Allen, postal pioneer, quarry magnate and owner of most of the land in Bathampton and Claverton parishes in the 18th Century.

Claverton Pumping Station

The pumping station is open to visitors at certain weekends and holidays. Its huge pumps deliver water from the river into the canal to maintain the water level.

Parking: Devonshire Road off Down Lane

Starting Point: Scout Hall opposite the top of Down Lane on the A36

Grid Ref: Parking: OS775:662
Start: OS776:659 Explorer Map155

Distance: Main route - 8.5 kms/5.3 miles
Monkton Combe extension -12.2 kms/7.6 miles

Approximate time: 2 hrs 40 mins or 4 hrs with extension to Monkton Combe.

Total Ascent: 175 metres or 215 metres

Summary:

One fairly steep ascent and descent , otherwise mostly flat. Extensive views over the Avon Valley and the City of Bath.

There is an extension to this route which takes in the village of Monkton Combe and part of the Somerset Coal Canal.

❊ *= See 'Points of Note' at the end of this walk.*

An impressive viaduct carries the A36 main road over school playing fields at Limpley Stoke near Monkton Combe and the junction of the Somerset Coal and Kennet & Avon canals.

Let's Go!

● Leaving the Scout Hall, head uphill on the bridleway which leads in a southerly direction, through a gate (6'). Continue up the bridleway between high banks until you see a Skyline Walk post on your left (8'). Carry on uphill for 30 metres as the ground starts to level out. The bridleway curves sharply left uphill towards the golf course but you should continue straight on with an escarpment on your right for 300 metres (7'). Go through a gateway with a metal stile, joining a track with woods on your right (4').

Walk on past the communication masts and the golf course fairways on your left (more details in Walk 3) until you arrive at the Golf Club car park. Cross it and pass behind the Club House and, keeping the next car park to your left, go straight ahead to Sham Castle, the creation of Bath's richest man in the 18th Century, Ralph Allen (15').

● Passing in front of Sham Castle enter a field. Follow a footpath along the left side of the field alongside a line of young trees. In the far corner cross a stone stile which leads to a footbridge over the Quarry Road approach to Bath University (5'). Keep straight on with a wall to your right. A small car park is reached and then a road where you turn right (5'). This brings you to Bathwick Hill. Taking care, cross over to a road (Copseland) that leads to another road, Widcombe Hill. Cross it with care and follow a lane straight ahead between the houses. This narrows to a footpath (6'). Follow this as it skirts more beech woods and continue straight ahead, ignoring all side paths.

The path leads to a gap in a wall (10') and heads onwards with a fence on your left until you re-enter the woods by a defunct kissing gate. The grounds of Klondyke House are on your left (6').

● Continue in a straight line with playing fields on your right. Just before the playing fields end and further woods are met, look for a kissing gate and National Trust Skyline footpath on your left (5'). Take this path through mixed woodland. At this point you may opt for the extended walk to Monkton Combe.

(Walk 5 continues overleaf)

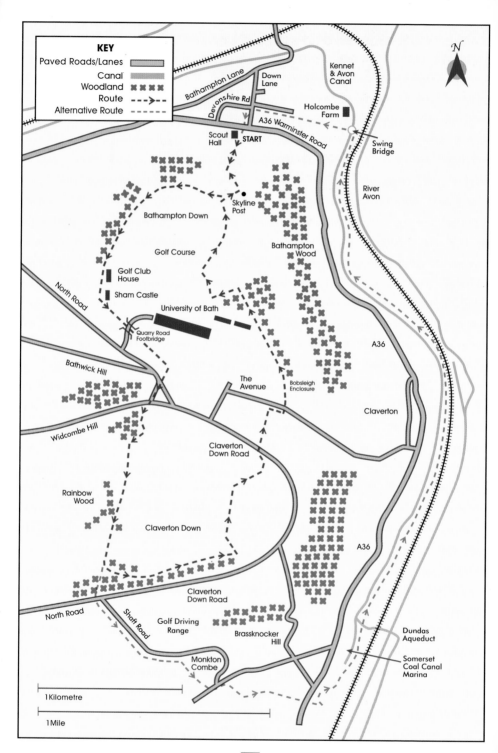

Alternative route via Monkton Combe village and the Somerset Coal Canal *

● *Ignore the NT Skyline path to the left and carry straight on until you come to a metalled road (Claverton Down Road). Taking care, cross, and follow the road ahead (Shaft Road). After passing a playing field on your right and a golf practice range on your left the road starts to drop downhill and grand views over the Avon and Midford valleys open up. Ignore two paths on your right but continue on downhill and look for a path on your right immediately past 'Prospect Cottage' (12').*

A short section of the Somerset Coal Canal has been restored and made into a marina at Monkton Combe.

Take this path which leads steeply down to Monkton Combe. On reaching the road, turn left (5'). At the end of the school buildings on your right and opposite the tennis courts (4'), take a cycle/footpath on your right for 100 metres. Then follow a PF branch to the left which drops down to a road which was formerly a railway line. Cross this and turn left along a path. Cross the entrance to the cricket field (5'). Descend a flight of steps and follow the footpath around the left-hand side of the cricket field, under the viaduct and over a stile out onto the Winsley road. Take great care crossing the road and 20 metres to the left, enter the approach to the Visitor Centre of the old Somerset Coal Canal (11'). Mount the ramp up to the canal marina. Turn left to the Visitor centre or right to continue. Walk along with the canal on your left until you find you have to take a path to the right where the towpath is closed to walkers. By following this path you soon arrive at the Dundas Aqueduct. There you join the Kennet and Avon Canal towpath (7'). Don't cross the Aqueduct but turn left, over the bridge across the SCC and follow the basin around to a footbridge which you cross. Then turn left and follow the towpath back towards Bathampton.*

When the swing bridge at Hampton Wharf is reached (1 hr 40'), cross the bridge and go through the kissing gate to the left of the private gate. Go up the path until it emerges into a lane which you follow until you reach Holcombe Lane. Walk past the shops to the T-junction where you join Down Lane. There you turn left, passing Devonshire Road on your right and a short distance ahead is the Warminster Road and your starting point (20').

Remaining with the basic route and ignoring the Monkton Combe alternative

● The route continues past some buildings on the right and meets a path coming in from the right. Ignore this and keep straight on. Go through a gap in the wall. At the end of the woods and before the back of a row of houses this path meets with another path (12'). Turn left, through a kissing gate, and, keeping the wall to your right, continue until the path splits into two.

● Take the right-hand path, passing through a kissing gate and onwards between a wall and a fence. Follow the path ahead

(Walk 5 continues overleaf)

through three kissing gates and eventually onto Claverton Down Road, adjacent to Bramley Cottages (16'). Cross the road and turn left, pass a bungalow (The Hollies) and immediately there is a path to your right, between a hedge and wall. Follow this as it skirts playing fields to the right and the RSPCA Dogs and Cats Home on your left and comes out onto a road called 'The Avenue'. Cross it and turn right for a short distance then take the first gate on your left onto a public bridleway (8').

● The way ahead passes the embankment of a rugby pitch on your left and a fenced enclosure on your right which contains a bobsleigh run used for training purposes. Keep the fence to your right, pass through some beech trees and then follow a wall on your right in a straight direction alongside playing fields and then on a gravel path past University buildings until it reaches a golf course (14'). Turn left and after 200 metres you come to a signposted junction (2'). Turn right onto a bridleway across part of the golf course. Pass alongside a steel fence on your right that protects a reservoir, and then through a clump of trees. Now head northwards across two fairways - being watchful not to cross in front of golfers actively engaged in play. The bridleway goes down a short slope to another fairway and straight ahead to a gate (10'). Continue downhill following a slightly shallow old track towards woods. Here you will rejoin the early part of the walk. Carry on down the bridleway to the start of the walk (18').

POINTS OF NOTE

The Somerset Coal Canal

The title says it all. This canal was backed by the owners of the many small collieries which operated in Somerset in the 19th century. By constructing the canal from the heart of the coalfield at Paulton, coal could be transported by barge to the Kennet and Avon Canal which in turn could convey it to Bristol and London and the Midlands through the network of canals that was being established in the early years of the century.

It opened to traffic in 1811, one year after the completion of the Kennet and Avon. For the next 60 years over 100,000 tons of coal were transported annually along the SCC making it a very profitable enterprise. Unfortunately for its fortunes, the spread of the railway network into Somerset saw coal hauliers preferring to use rail transport. Traffic on the SCC declined rapidly and by the 1890s the canal company was bankrupt. The canal finally closed in 1901, In 1904 the Great Western Railway bought it for the Camerton to Limpley Stoke extension. Now the only part that is open is the short stretch used as a marina which you see on this walk.

William Smith (1769 - 1839) who founded the modern science of geology was the surveyor/engineer in charge of the construction of the canal for six years when he lived at Tucking Mill, Midford. His observations of the geology of this area through which the canal was cut led him to formulate his ideas on rock strata which culminated in his book "The Order of Strata" and his geological maps of Britain which were the foundation stones of modern geology.

Starting Point: Junction of Bathampton Lane and the A36 (Bath-Warminster Road)

Grid Ref: OS768:659 Explorer Map155

Distance: 9.75 kms/6 miles

Approximate time: 3 hours

Total Ascent: 340 metres

Summary:
Three steep ascents and descents around the southern downs of Bath. They bring their reward - superb views over the City and interesting sights along the route. Return by the canal towpath. A challenge for fit walkers.

✷ *= See 'Points of Note' at the end of this walk.*

Let's Go!

● Leave the A36 opposite the junction of the A36 and Bathampton Lane by taking the track uphill at the entrance to St. George's Hill. Pass the pumping station on your right and go through the kissing gate.

Go straight up the broad track for about half a kilometre until you reach a gate (12'). Go through it and continue up a grassy slope past a waymark post after which you will turn right and go through a gateway with the fence and woods on your right (2'). When the track peters out go straight ahead over the grass, veering away from the woods towards the right of the communication masts. Just after passing them you rejoin a broad track. The woods and the fence are on your right. Carry on along this track until you reach a stile (11'). Cross the car park, then past the rear of the Golf Club buildings, through a second car park and onto the start of a clearing in front of Sham Castle. Here, look right for a small path cutting downhill through woods for 50 metres to the Golf Club access road. Cross the road to a lay-by with a bench which gives a marvellous view over Bath (5').

● 20 metres down the Golf Club access road is a kissing gate into National Trust land. Go through it and follow the path downhill keeping the fence line to your left. This leads to a kissing gate and steps which bring you to North Road and more opportunities for bird's eye views of the City. Cross the road and turn right (4').

Bath city centre and the Abbey from North Road.

(Walk 6 continues overleaf)

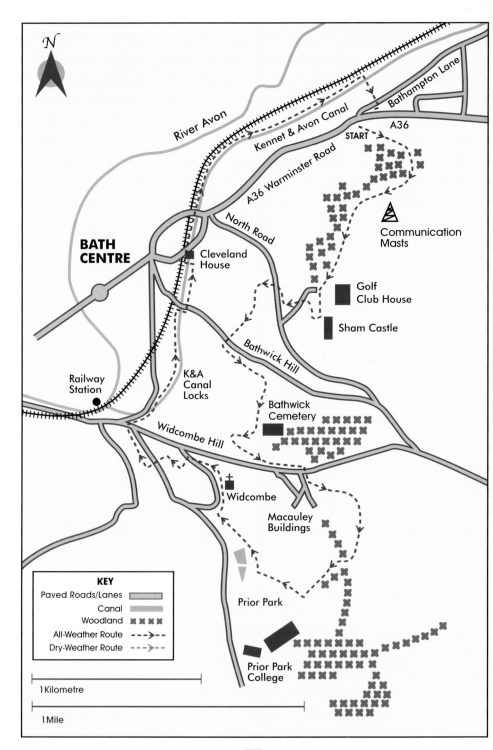

Follow the pavement downhill for about 150 metres, keeping an eye open for a flight of steps and footpath with a Skyline Walk post going off to your left between two fields. Take this path and having passed between two houses you reach Cleveland Walk (3'). Turn left and follow Cleveland Walk until its junction with Bathwick Hill. Taking care, cross Bathwick Hill and take the path ahead between the houses (5'). This quickly joins a cross path and more views - towards Beechen Cliff and the Lyncombe and Widcombe valleys. Smallcombe Vale is immediately ahead.

● Turn left and follow the path uphill, behind the large mansions of Bathwick Hill on your left and a field boundary fence on your right. At the end of this path there are two kissing gates on your right (6'). Take the furthest one which leads into a path downhill with fences on either side. This leads to a flight of steps, then through a gate where you bear left down to the valley bottom passing the delightful Smallcombe Farm and lake. Crossing the access road to Bathwick Cemetery, go through a kissing gate (5'). Follow the path as it slopes gradually uphill to your right, and at the far corner of the field pass through a kissing gate into the field above (5'). Turn left past a water trough and follow the path as it gradually slopes uphill away from the left-hand hedge and towards the opposite corner. Here there is a kissing gate leading into the next field and immediately another kissing gate on your right leading out onto Widcombe Hill road (12'). At the road turn left and walk uphill past Macaulay Buildings. Cross the road. Take a path through a gap in the wall just to the left of the large private entrance leading to Rainbow Wood House (4'). Follow the path uphill along the edge of woodland to the left and railings to the right.

● As this enclosed path leaves the woodland it levels out, passing between walls. After passing through a kissing gate another 'cross' path is encountered (7'). Turn right and after a while pass through a gap in a wall (3'). Carry on straight ahead with a fence on your left and about two-thirds of the way across this field there is a signed path going off to your right (3'). Follow this into woodland and descend a series of steps with metal railings on your right. Here you are entering the northern end of Rainbow Wood - so named as it is planted in the shape of a rainbow - and more outstanding views of Bath. Do not take the kissing gate in front of you at this point but turn left, keeping the railings on your right and Rainbow Wood to your left. Pass through two stone pillars, with more outstanding views of Bath from along this former 'ride' (7').

● Turn right at the pillars through a kissing gate and head downhill through another kissing gate in the hedge slightly to your right. Follow a well defined path downhill to your left, giving fine views of Prior Park Lake in winter. Cross a low metal stile in the far bottom corner of the field (4'). Descend steps to a path leading to Church Lane. Follow this lane and turn down steps to your left immediately after "The Dell" (4'). This path emerges into another lane, Church Street, alongside the outfall from the lake (3'). Cross it, turn right uphill and soon you will be admiring Widcombe Manor on your left and Thomas à Becket Church on your right. Continue along the lane as it bends left and just before it joins Widcombe Hill descend a short, steep flight of steps on your left (6'). Carry on downhill leaving Widcombe Crescent to your right.

● Take the lane ahead downhill past a Quaker burial site where it swings right behind Widcombe Crescent and in front of the mews. Look for another flight of steps (Widcombe Rise) on your left which leads down to Prior Park Road (3').

(Walk 6 continues overleaf)

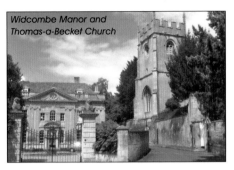

Widcombe Manor and Thomas-a-Becket Church

Cross this road, turn right and immediately take a little path to your left which follows the front of Prior Park Buildings alongside the stream we encountered earlier. Continue until the stream disappears and a lane crosses your path. Go straight across it and along a service lane between walls. Bear first right down the slope of Millbrook Place, which brings you to Widcombe High Street (3'). Using the pedestrian crossing, cross over and follow the pavement to your right until it reaches the canal bridge. Take the path to your left just before the bridge. You now have the opportunity of continuing ahead to explore the lock system at the point where the canal joins the river.

● The walk proper continues by turning sharp right at the canal side to pass under the bridge, up steps and over a walkway which takes you over the lock. Turn right onto the towpath (3').

● Arriving at Horseshoe Bridge you cannot pass under the arch so it is necessary to cross over the road at this point. It is not possible to go under the bridge at Bathwick Hill either. At this point the towpath changes sides. Take the steps to the left of the bridge, and turn right to cross the bridge. Then immediately cross over Bathwick Hill and the towpath is directly ahead of you and leads to Cleveland House - uniquely built over a canal tunnel.

This building was formerly the HQ of the Kennet & Avon Canal Company

● On reaching the house turn left by taking the path along the side of Cleveland House and descend steps which lead down to the towpath on the other side of the canal. This path takes you under the house and through Sydney Gardens, where it is possible to leave the canal side for a while to explore this delightful park.

The towpath leaves the gardens through another tunnel and gradually the canal winds away from the City into more open countryside and wide valley views.

● This walk leaves the canal at the next stone bridge, locally known as 'Candy's Bridge' by taking the stone stile just before the bridge and turning right, through a gate into Meadow Farm Lane. Turn right and follow the lane up to the junction with Bathampton Lane; here turn right to reach the starting point (60').

POINTS OF NOTE

Prior Park and Gardens

Bath's greatest entrepreneur, Ralph Allen (1693 – 1774) commissioned John Wood the Elder (1704 – 1754) in 1742 to design this mansion overlooking Bath. The Palladian splendour reminds us of Wood's other creations that contribute to Bath's famed Georgian architecture such as The Circus, Queen's Square and North and South Parades. Prior Park is now a Roman Catholic secondary school for boarders and day pupils.

Ralph Allen was advised on the design of the gardens by the great 18th century landscaper, Capability Brown and by the poet, Alexander Pope. Its most splendid feature is the Palladian bridge flanked by two lakes. The gardens are owned by the National Trust and are open throughout the year to the public.

Parking/Starting Point:
a.Unmetalled section of the George car park
b. Opposite The Crown, Bathford

Grid Ref: OS776:665 (a); 787:669(b)
Explorer Map155
Distance: 12.5 kms/8 miles
Approximate time: 4 hours
Total Ascent: 255 metres

Summary:
One steep ascent to Brown's Folly and a descent, steep in parts, to the River Avon and the Dundas Aqueduct. An easy return by the Kennet & Avon Canal towpath.

✤ = *See 'Points of Note' at the end of this walk.*

Let's Go!

● Leaving the car park, carefully cross the road and go through the gate into the churchyard. Cross it in front of the main door of the church and exit via a metal gate. Cross the lane and go past the front of Bathampton Primary School into Tyning Road. This road leads eastwards until it reaches a railway crossing. Only cross the track when the light is on. Descend the steps on the other side of the track. The path is straight ahead, slightly veering to the left towards a kissing gate in the far corner of the field and then onto a path alongside the railway line but separated from it by a high diamond-mesh fence. It crosses the River Avon and joins the A363, the Bath to Bradford-on-Avon Road (15').

Cross this road with care, turn right and over a pedestrian bridge that spans the By Brook. At the road junction take Ostlings Lane, just to the right of The Crown pub (3').

Brown's Folly or 'The Pepperpot'

Follow this lane uphill and around to the left until you come into Church Lane. Cross it and take the path opposite which slopes up to the lych gate of St. Swithun's Church✤ (7').

● Turn left at the lych gate and up some steps to follow a path on the left of the churchyard. This leads to Pump Lane alongside the impressive Manor Tithe Barn. Cross the lane diagonally into Mountain Wood. Keeping to the right-hand side of this road, look out for a path that leads up onto the right-hand grassy bank and for a stile in the hedge on your right, near the houses ahead. Climb this stile and follow a path which slopes diagonally up to the woods. Here there is another stile leading into the woods and an information board (10').

● Take the wide path in front of you that leads uphill. After a while this becomes a well worn 'sunken' route and eventually meets a track at a T- junction (5'). Turn left and follow the track for approximately 150 metres. Look to your right for another track which makes a tight "V." Take this track which turns in the direction from which you have come. Follow this to a gate and kissing gate. This track gradually slopes upward through scrubland to a fence and another kissing gate. Do not go through the kissing gate, and ignore steps which follow the fence steeply uphill. Instead turn sharp left to follow a narrow path which skirts the edge of old quarries.

This path gives the best opportunity to enjoy far reaching views of the Avon valley and the Downs to the south, west and north.

(Walk 7 continues overleaf)

27

Leave the path where it comes to a fence and kissing gate and turn right up a steep flight of steps to the hill top. At the top go immediately right through the kissing gate and straight ahead until Brown's Folly※ is reached (15').

● The walk now leads southwards from Brown's Folly along the top of the slope through woods with a wall on your left until you arrive at an information panel. Ignore the path to your left and continue with the wall on your left on flat ground.

Parts of it are rough with stones and tree roots and can be muddy. Ignore the path back to the right. The route leaves the wall and descends to the right. It needs to be walked with care. As the path approaches the Bath - Bradford on Avon Road (A363) it turns left to a stile. Having climbed the stile, keep straight ahead until you reach the road (25'). Keep to the left-hand verge (stay well away from the road edge as this is a busy road) and follow this to a cottage (Dry Arch House). Take the bridleway on the right of the cottage gateway and within a few metres go right, under the road, to a stone stile in the wall ahead where the bridleway turns slightly left, and there is a gateway to your right (3').

● Cross the stile and walk downhill through woods with a broken wall on your right The path continues downhill between hedges. In winter or after wet weather this can be uneven and muddy. Continue down a steep slope, through a kissing gate and into Warleigh Lane with Hanover Square Cottage nearby (8').

The route turns left up the lane to Sheephouse Farm. Turn right through the farmyard to a permissive footpath between two gates at the end of the right-hand range of low farm buildings (5'). Follow this downhill, between two fences, and cross another stile.

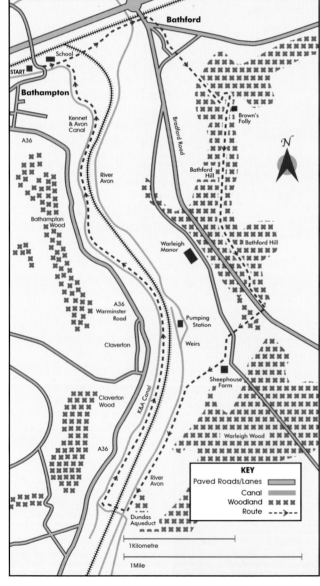

Carry on downhill with a fence on your left for 40 metres until you meet and cross a stile.

The path now gradually slopes down between bramble bushes and scrub to the banks of the River Avon. The path swings left in a southerly direction across three fields alongside the river towards the Dundas Aqueduct[*]. At the field boundaries use the wooden footbridges to avoid getting wet feet!

Dundas Aqueduct carries the Kennet & Avon Canal over the river Avon.

The last hedge has a stile in it and from here on you get grand views of Dundas Aqueduct. The path veers to the left of the boathouses to a stile on the other side of which a long flight of steps leads up to the canal towpath. Turn right and take your time to cross the Aqueduct because from it you will enjoy magnificent views of the river and its wooded banks (25').

● Take the towpath back to Bathampton. On the way you will pass Claverton Pumping Station which was opened in 1814 to pump water from the River Avon to the canal. Half a mile from Bathampton there is a wooden swing bridge at Hampton Wharf, now a mooring for some narrowboats. In the past it was the terminal, completed in 1808, for a tramway that carried wagon-loads of stone from the quarries on Bathampton Down to the canal. The stone was loaded onto barges which carried it west to Bath and Bristol and east to various destinations. Continue along the towpath to your starting point beside 'The George" (2 hrs 20').

POINTS OF NOTE

St. Swithun's Church

The church was rebuilt and extended

between 1870 and 1880 but it stands on the site of much older and smaller churches first referred to in 1170. In the churchyard is a stone chest tomb of Anne Nelson, sister of Admiral Lord Nelson. It stands under a spreading yew, the inscription still clearly showing her name and date of death, 15th November 1783, aged 23.

Brown's Folly

Brown's Folly, or the "Pepperpot", was built in 1848 by Mr Wade Brown who owned the local quarry. Like most follies, such as Sham Castle, it was built to be seen. The initials of Wade Brown appear above the entrance door with the date of construction, 1848. Below it are the initials CH and the date 1907 because by then the estate belonged to Sir Charles Hobhouse.

Dundas Aqueduct

Dundas Aqueduct takes its name from Charles Dundas, chairman of the Kennet and Avon Canal Company, which in 1794 began the construction of the canal. The engineer in charge was John Rennie, and it was he who designed this aqueduct as well as its sister at Avoncliff some two miles to the south. The Aqueduct was completed in 1800.

Parking/Starting Point:
a.Unmetalled section of the George car park
b.Opposite The Crown, Bathford
Grid Ref: OS776:665 (a); 787:669(b)
Explorer Maps 155 and 156
Distance: 9.8 kms/6.1 miles
Approximate time: 3 hours
Total Ascent: 220 metres

Summary:

A fairly level walk apart from an ascent to Kingsdown from Bathford.

❖ = See 'Points of Note' at the end of this walk.

Let's Go!

● Leaving the car park, carefully cross the road and go through the gate into the churchyard. Cross it in front of the main door of the church and exit via a metal gate. Cross the lane and go past the front of Bathampton Primary School into Tyning Road. This road leads eastwards until it reaches a railway crossing. Only cross the track when the light is on. Descend the steps on the other side of the track. The path is straight ahead, slightly veering to the left towards a kissing gate in the far corner of the field and then onto a path alongside the railway line but separated from it by a high diamond-mesh fence. It crosses the River Avon and joins the A363, the Bath to Bradford-on-Avon Road (15').

Cross carefully, turn right, walk over the wooden bridge across the By Brook and continue until opposite the Crown. Go left and up Bathford Hill into Bathford village.

Opposite the first turning to your left is the Bathford Lock-up, built in 1820 but replaced in 1837. It has two cells, one of which served as village mortuary until 1924. It has the original iron studded doors with fittings and grilles.

● With the shop/post office on your right, take the turning to your left, Ashley Road (10'). Follow it until it becomes a rough bridleway. Continue on this bridleway crossing a stream by means of a wooden walkway until the bridleway swings left about 0.5km beyond the stream. Here turn right

on to the signed footpath which goes through a gate (28'). Go up the hill keeping the hedge to your right until you come to Ashley Wood Farm, then go through the gate leading onto a driveway. Go straight on, keeping the farm and outhouses to your left. This leads onto a lane (10').Turn left and keep straight on along Lower Kingsdown Road.

● At the T-junction go straight over and up the footpath ahead (7'). At Kingsdown Golf Course it becomes a gravelled pathway. Follow this as it goes uphill and bears right through trees to meet a T-junction. Here, cross the fairway, veering slightly right in front of a tee. The entrance to the path is slightly difficult to find but it leads down through woods to steps onto the Bathford - Kingsdown Road. Cross this road with care and take the track opposite. After 50m, bear left and after a further 100m, enter a field (10').

Bathford lock-up

● Carry straight on with the hedge on your right and cross a stile next to a gate. Continue through the next field with the hedge to your left. At the corner of the wall cross the field diagonally to the right of a pylon and pond in the far corner of the field. Cross the stile ahead and walk between woods and a hedge. On leaving the wood continue across a field now keeping the hedge on your left until you reach a lane (17').

Cross this and take the track ahead, between hedges. After 80m, cross a stile into a field keeping the hedge on your left until you come to another lane (6'). On this part of the walk there are fine views southwards towards Salisbury Plain and the Westbury White Horse. Turn right up the lane to Home Farm. You can take a break by following the lane to Monkton Farleigh which has a pub and a church.

The Monks' Conduit

● Take the track to the right of Home Farm. Where this metalled track ends, cross a stile (3'). Continue straight on, gently uphill, along a footpath between fields.

Note the old low stone building known as the Monks' Conduit on your left. This was built to protect the spring from which the monks obtained their water supply.

● Cross a road and go straight ahead along a track with a hedge on the right. Cross a stile with a fence on your left and continue to a lane (7'). Cross the lane and walk 100m through a copse to a metalled track. Turn left on the track and soon, as the track swings left, leave it and bear ahead across the middle of a field towards a gate. Go through the gate onto a woodland path between two low walls and you soon reach a notice at the entrance to Brown's Folly Nature Reserve (5'). This consists of 30 acres of land overlooking the valley of the River Avon and maintained by the Avon Wildlife Trust. Turn right at this point.

The path now runs very close to the wall and soon you will pass Brown's Folly on your right (5') (see Walk 7 for details of the Folly).

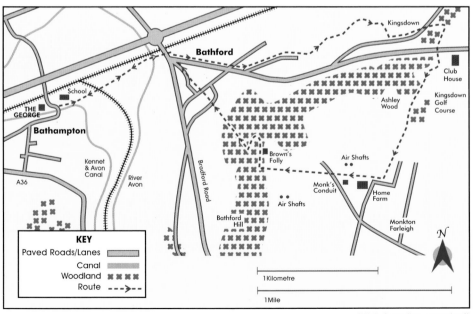

KEY

Paved Roads/Lanes	
Canal	
Woodland	✖ ✖ ✖ ✖
Route	- - ->- -

1 Kilometre

1 Mile

(Walk 8 continues overleaf)

● Continue straight on past the Folly, a metal fence on your left. At its end is a kissing gate. Go through this and descend a flight of steep steps. At the bottom, turn left and follow the path along the edge of a steep drop. This gives the most magnificent views of the surrounding countryside (see Walk No 7). The path eventually comes to a metal fence directly below The Folly and another kissing gate. Ignore it and turn sharp right heading for another kissing gate. Pass through the gate, follow the track to a junction with another track and turn sharp left. Continue looking for a path leading off to your right. Go along this path for about 200 metres until you reach one going downhill to your right which is waymarked with the 'Pepperpot Trail' symbol (15').

● Turn right and follow this path downhill to a stile and another Information Board (5'). Cross the field ahead as the path slants slightly to your right to a stile in a hedge next to houses. Turn left down a grass bank into Mountain Wood Road and continue downhill to its junction with Pump Lane (10'). Cross it, turn right, and take a lane to the left between an old cottage and a tithe barn. Walk down to the church and steps that lead to the lych gate. Turn right into Church Lane (2').

The Parish Church of St Swithun Bathford has a statue of the patron saint in the niche of the tower of the church. It has a Norman doorway and font and a Jacobean pulpit. The tomb of Lord Nelson's sister is in the churchyard.

● Cross into Ostlings Lane. Follow this taking the right hand bend as it passes Church Close. This lane eventually comes to The Crown Public House (on your right) and the junction of Bathford Hill and the A363. Taking great care cross over to the pavement ahead (6').

● In order to return to Bathampton it is now necessary to retrace the first section of the outgoing route (18').

Looking towards Bathford with the village and church on the left and Brown's Folly on the skyline, top right.

Starting Point: Batheaston village car park (free for up to 3 hours) or the paying car park behind The George & Dragon.

Grid Ref: OS780:674 Explorer Map 155

Distance: 8.8 kms/5.5 miles

Approximate time: 3 hours

Total Ascent: 276 metres

Summary:

A fairly steep ascent from the starting point and later on a long descent into St Catherine's Valley. A further short ascent is followed by a gentle descent to St Catherine's Court and Church followed by a mainly level walk back to Batheaston along lanes and footpaths.

✻ *= See 'Points of Note' at the end of this walk.*

Let's Go!

The Batheaston Car Park is situated on the east side of the village opposite a line of shops on the main road, between the road and the River Avon. For parking, see above.

● Cross the main road by the pedestrian crossing, bearing right to Fosse Lane. Walk up Fosse Lane to the end of the tarmac and go straight on up a track passing a large house on your left. About 300 metres beyond it there is a PF sign pointing left (22').

● Descend the path along the left-hand edge of two fields, heading for the bottom left-hand corner to a tarmac road (Steway Lane). Turn right up the road for a about half a mile till you come to a footpath sign pointing left. The very faint path leads you down the fields close to the left-hand field hedge until you come to St Catherine's Brook (30').

● Follow this upstream, the brook on your left, until you come to a track. Turn left over a grass-covered stone bridge across the brook and immediately turn right over a stile. Cross the field and make for the stile, to the left of a yard, on to a road. Turn right along the road, cross a bridge and in 50 yards climb a stile into the field on your left (15'). Follow the brook, which is again on your left.

● At the end of the field, cross a stile, a drive and another stile and proceed straight ahead to a driveway with a beech hedge on your left. You come to another drive and enter a field ahead of you by a stile where there is a sign telling you that you are on the 'Limestone Way' which links the Mendips to the Cotswolds (5'). The path keeps close to the brook, which is still on your left, and takes you to a gate and a concrete footbridge. Here there is a sign indicating a Permissive Path. Go straight uphill on the left of the farmhouse drive. At the first hedge go left, past a stile (<u>don't</u> cross it) to a power line, just before which you take a path following the general direction of the power line slightly downhill to a (wobbly!) stile (20').

● Cross the stile carefully and proceed on a level path till you reach a belt of trees and a large manhole cover. Thereafter edge diagonally downhill towards the bottom corner by the brook. There are good views of St Catherine's Court✻ and vineyards from the path (8').

(Walk 9 continues overleaf)

St Catherine's Church

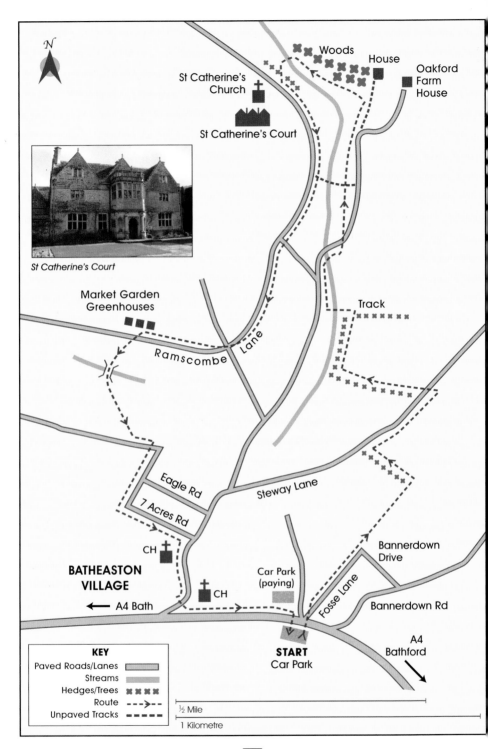

St Catherine's Court

N

Woods

House

Oakford Farm House

St Catherine's Church

St Catherine's Court

Track

Market Garden Greenhouses

Ramscombe Lane

Eagle Rd

7 Acres Rd

Steway Lane

CH

BATHEASTON VILLAGE

CH

Car Park (paying)

Bannerdown Drive

Fosse Lane

Bannerdown Rd

← A4 Bath

START
Car Park

A4 Bathford

KEY

Paved Roads/Lanes	
Streams	
Hedges/Trees	✖ ✖ ✖
Route	--->--
Unpaved Tracks	▄▄▄

½ Mile

1 Kilometre

● Cross a stile and immediately left over another stile and a bridge into a private garden. Bear sharp left keeping well away from the house to a kissing gate in the hedge and wend your way up through the next field to St Catherine's Church (3').

● Follow the lane past the Church (well worth a visit) and the Court until you come to a fork. Take the right-hand road, Ramscombe Lane, to a cross road. Continue straight on (still Ramscombe Lane) to a (easily missed) kissing gate with PF sign on your left opposite

St Catherine's Court

Captain William Blanchard, died 1631, and his wife, the second of five generations of Blanchards who owned St. Catherine's Court.

some greenhouses (35'). Go downhill, bearing right, to a gate in the middle of a fence. Continue on to a bridge over a brook, cross it and then walk uphill away from the brook along the left-hand edge of the field to find another gate onto a lane (10').

● Turn left and follow the lane (Seven Acres Lane), past a market garden and Eagle Road to 7 Acres Road. Here, turn left and at the foot turn right, past the parish church of St John the Baptist and the junction with Solsbury Lane. Continue until you reach the Church of the Good Shepherd. Just past the Church, take a footpath that descends to Batheaston's main street. To end the walk, go left past the shops to a pedestrian crossing with the free car park on the far side or around the corner to your left for the paying car park (30').

POINTS OF NOTE

St Catherine's Court and Church

St Catherine's Court was the manor house of an extensive estate which belonged to Bath Abbey from at least 1086 when it is mentioned in the Domesday Book. By 1310 it belonged to the Prior of Bath Priory up to the Dissolution of the Monasteries in 1539. The manor house was used as a retreat by the Prior. From the estate the Priory obtained meat and wool from the sheep, flour from the estate's mill, wine from its vineyards and fish from its fish ponds.

After 1539, St Catherine's Court and the estate became the property of Henry VIII. He sold it to his tailor and from then on it was in the ownership of a succession of families who over the next five centuries changed, extended and modernised the Court and the adjoining church.

Although St Catherine's Court and its grounds are private, St Catherine's Church is open to the public and is accessed through the main entrance gate to the Court. The Church is well worth a visit, with unusual ceramic tile panels, old stained glass windows and interesting family memorials.

Starting Point: Batheaston village car parks opposite and behind the George & Dragon

Grid Ref: OS787:669

Explorer Maps 155 and 156

Alternative Starting Points:

a.Unmetalled section of The George car park

b.Opposite The Crown, Bathford

Grid Ref: a. OS776:665   b. OS787:669

Explorer Maps 155 and 156

Distance:

From Batheaston or Bathford: 8 kms/5 miles

From Bathampton: 10.4 kms/6.5 miles

Approximate time:

From Batheaston or Bathford: 2 hrs 40 mins

From Bathampton: 3 hrs 10 mins

Total Ascent: (all starting points) 200 metres

Summary:

A pleasant level walk from Bathampton through the By Brook Valley to Shockerwick. From there a steady uphill walk on roads and footpaths up to Bannerdown. From Bannerdown Common the views are excellent. The descent into Batheaston is fairly gradual.

Let's Go!

● Leave the car park and follow the road (London Road East) to the right towards Bathford. Just before the roundabout, take the underpass below the A4 Bypass, then continue under the railway bridge on the A363 Bath to Bradford-on-Avon road (10').

Alternative Start from Bathampton

● *Leave the George car park and cross the road with care into the churchyard. Go through the churchyard past the church and exit via a metal gate turning right and then left into Tyning Road. Pass the Primary School and proceed along Tyning Road until it ends at the level crossing. Cross carefully and only when the light is on. Descend the steps on the opposite side and follow the path across the pastures towards a pylon before the railway embankment. Go through a kissing gate, up the side of the embankment and cross the River Avon on the railway bridge. Drop down to the A363 to join the main walk (15').*

Cross the road carefully and turn right over the By Brook by the footbridge.

● Bear left up Bathford Hill past the Crown Inn and the lock-up referred to in Walk 8. Bear left just after the Bathford Post Office onto Ashley Road (10'). Follow this until it degenerates into a rough bridleway. Soon you cross a stream by a wooden footbridge (20'). The bridleway climbs and in 100 metres from the stream veers right. At this point, just before a gate into a field, turn left through the undergrowth and trees to reach a stile (2').

Go over the stile then sharp right along the top edge of two fields with the hedge on your right for 300 metres. Go through the gate and bear diagonally downhill to a group of farm buildings. To the right of them is an open gate and broken stile. Go through the gate, and within 40 metres there is a stile on your left. Cross it and over a farm track to another stile. Go over the stile and descend a set of steps down to a track. Turn right to the gate and on to the tarmac road (15'). Continue up the road, passing the entrance to Sheylors Farm on the

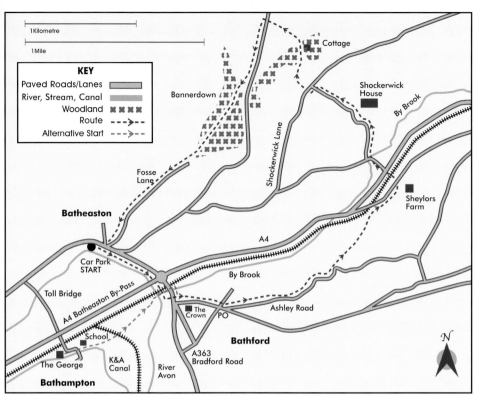

KEY

Paved Roads/Lanes	
River, Stream, Canal	
Woodland	✖ ✖ ✖
Route	- - -➤- -
Alternative Start	- - -➤- -

right and after a further 100m, opposite 'Home Orchard', take a path to the left (5'). Descend to a footbridge and cross the railway line (3').

● Cross the main A4 road here with great care and go down the side road signposted to Shockerwick. Cross the By Brook and take the first road to the right (5'). Follow the lane uphill past a row of houses and then the entrance to Shockerwick House. Continue up the lane to the junction with Shockerwick Lane and turn left (20').

After 80m, at Shockerwick Farm (1'), follow the Byway sign to your right. It indicates a track that winds up the hill to a cottage. From various points on this section of the walk, pause to catch your breath and enjoy the view. Continue uphill past the cottage, through a belt of woodland until you emerge into high farmland and carry straight on to the Batheaston to Colerne road. It's as straight as a die at this point, part of the Roman Fosse Way that linked Bath to Cirencester (20').

● Cross the road with care. Turn left walking on the verge and after 500 metres there is a lay-by on the right (7'). Go through the gate and onto Bannerdown Common and traverse the open common on the bridleway south toward Bath. Where you have a choice of paths, keep to the right and start dropping downhill in a south west direction through intermittent woodland. The path widens within a narrow strip of woodland with a wall on your left (20'). The bridleway passes houses on your left. Ignore all cross-paths and go straight ahead to a tarmac lane (Fosse Lane) which goes steeply downhill in a straight line emerging at the foot of Bannerdown Rd by the roundabout opposite the village car park starting point (20').

● If you started from Bathampton or Bathford, cross the main road at the pelican crossing and turn left following it to the roundabout. Take the underpass beneath the A4 by-pass, go under the railway bridge and either continue straight ahead to The Crown or turn right on the PF to Bathampton (25').

37

Parking/Starting Point:
Unmetalled section of The George car park
Grid Ref: OS776:665 Explorer Map 155
Distance: 12 kms/7.5 miles
Approximate time: 4 hours 20 minutes
Total Ascent: 450 metres

Summary:
This is the toughest and longest walk in the book. It involves three quite long ascents to each of the three hills, Bannerdown, Holt Down and Little Solsbury. In winter or after spells of wet weather some parts of the walk can be quite muddy. However, the views from the tops of these hills are the best in this area, especially those from Little Solsbury. Walkers who undertake this strenuous day's walk will feel it has been very worthwhile.

Let's Go!

● Leaving the car park, carefully cross the road and go through the gate into the churchyard. Cross it in front of the main door of the church and exit via a metal gate. Cross the lane and go past the front of Bathampton Primary School into Tyning Road. This road leads eastwards until it reaches a railway crossing. Only cross the track when the light is on. Descend the steps on the other side of the track. The path is straight ahead, slightly veering to the left through a kissing gate and towards a pylon. Go through the kissing gate and up a path alongside the railway line but separated from it by a high diamond mesh fence. It crosses the River Avon and joins the A363, the Bath to Bradford-on-Avon Road (15').

● Cross the road carefully and turn right towards the Crown Inn. Turn left up Bathford Hill into Bathford village. Take the second road on the left immediately after a BT telephone box. After 100m, at the end of a high wall on the left, take a path left downhill, through a kissing gate and down a field to the right hand end of the paper mill.

Go through a kissing gate, cross the By Brook and walk under the railway bridge to the main A4, opposite Bathford Nursery (15').

Cross the road with care and turn right. Just before the second house turn left up a driveway and after 40 metres join a footpath between a hedge and a solid wooden fence.

Follow the footpath uphill for 20 metres, cross a stile, go over a farm track and across a second stile. Continue uphill with a hedge on your left, over a stile and past some farm sheds. Still with a hedge on your left, join an old tarmac track uphill through a gate up to Shockerwick Lane (10').

● Cross a stone stile and turn right for 230m, then left over a wooden stile with a PF sign. Proceed straight up the slope with the field boundary hedge and telephone line on your right. A set of wooden steps in the top corner of the field leads to the Colerne road (15'). Cross it carefully.

The path goes sharply to the right just before a metal gate. Proceed uphill between a wall and bank ignoring paths to the right until you come to a T-junction (8'). Turn right uphill, leaving the official footpath for 20m then cut left for another 20m and left again onto the flat Common of Bannerdown. There is woodland on your left and scrub trees on your right. Continue along the left-hand fringe of the Common for about 200m. Then walk a further 200m towards the centre of the Common with a communication mast ahead of you.

Here, you meet a cross path and turn left towards the left-hand (western) woods. Just before the corner of the Common you will see a PF sign pointing you north west down through the woods. Ignore a path to the left and soon join a track to a house. Turn right up the track to Steway Lane (15').

● Almost straight across the Lane is a PF sign to the path that takes a long descent downhill between two field boundaries (10'). At the foot, cross a stile and walk 40m straight ahead. Here, turn left and follow a sunken track downhill with a hedge to your right and cross St Catherine's Brook (4').

● Turn right immediately over a stile and follow the brook upstream keeping left of a fenced timber yard. Cross a stile into a metalled lane. Turn right past a waterworks plant, across a bridge, and straightaway cross a stile on your left. The path goes across a meadow, through a gate with the Brook on your left. At the far end go over a stile, across a lane, then over another stile. Shortly, take a driveway to your left crossing over the brook (despite appearances this is a right of way). Go straight ahead some 30m to a footpath between two houses. This path is often muddy and overgrown and is accessed by a metal gate. The path winds up to St Catherine's Lane. Turn left along the lane for 60m. Go right for 10m and then up the "Byway" just before the gate to "Holt Barn" (5').

(Walk 11 continues overleaf)

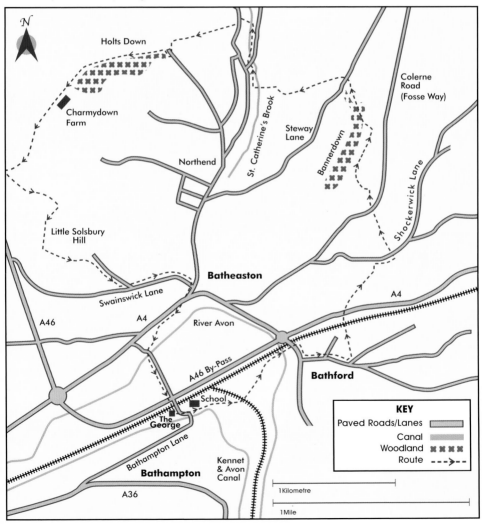

Ahead of you is the longest, steepest part of the walk as you ascend from St. Catherine's Valley to the second hill, Holts Down. When you emerge onto a lane at the top of the path you are rewarded with wonderful views to the east and south (25') The cottage here is called "Down Edge".

● Walk left along the flat track to a fork and go right uphill. Then after 60 metres, at a junction of a PF and a bridleway, go left through a gate. Follow the footpath as it curves around the southern (left hand) edge of fields through two metal gates until you reach Charmydown Farm (20').

With the farm buildings and the fence to your left, continue along the PF to the corner of the field. Here, cross a wooden stile over the fence on your left onto a track. Go down it for 40m to a junction and go right. After 120m, climb a stile on your left onto a road and turn right. After a further 50 metres, cross a stile on your left into a field (5').

Follow the PF diagonally downhill with a line of wooden poles to your left. After 200m, just before the field edge, turn sharp left under the line of poles for about 30m and cross a stile on your right (5').

The PF continues diagonally downhill for 130 metres to a hedge with the line of poles on your right.(3') Here, cross a stile and descend a flight of 100 steps cut into the steep wooded hillside. Go carefully; cross a stile and descend a few more steps before you come to open ground. Go diagonally downhill to a semi-ruined stone shelter and through a metal gate (12').

Follow the bridleway uphill to your right past a post with a bridleway sign to a steep wooded slope and cross a stile at the top of a short flight of steps (7').

Once over the stile, turn left uphill along the left-hand edge of the field to a wooden gate. The PF continues straight ahead to another wooden gate (14'). Here there is an information panel about Little Solsbury Hill which is owned by the National Trust. It is Open Access Land, so you can roam over it.

Walk straight uphill through a cleft in a high, grassy bank where you emerge onto a level plateau. Turn right along the ridge overlooking the ancient defensive ditch that encircles the hill. There are magnificent views in all directions. It is easy to appreciate why this was such a prime location for a fortified village in pre-Roman days (7').

Little Solsbury Hill

● Leave the Hill by a path on the south-east side dropping to a farmhouse and a National Trust information board about Little Solsbury Hill. Go down steps, through a kissing gate to Solsbury Lane (10'). Follow it down until it meets Swainswick Lane where you turn left and follow on downhill into Batheaston. At the foot of Solsbury Lane (15'), turn right and keep to the raised pavement until you reach Batheaston High Street. Turn right and cross the road at the pelican crossing. Turn right and continue west for 200 metres until you reach a public footpath on the left. This path takes you downhill between houses and gardens to another path where you turn right. This path leads to the toll bridge where you will turn left. Cross the toll bridge and go along Mill Lane to the George and your start point (25").

Starting Point: Larkhall Inn or
Meadow Lane, Bathampton

Grid Ref: Larkhall: OS761:665
Meadow Lane: OS771:661
Explorer Map 155

● **Larkhall via Langridge:**

Distance: 11.3 kms /7 miles

Approximate time: 3 hours 45 minutes

Total Ascent: 350 metres

● **Larkhall - Woolley - Larkhall:**

Distance: 7.4 kms /4.7 miles

Approximate time: 2 hours 30 minutes

Total Ascent: 180 metres

*For Start/Finish from Meadow Lane,
Bathampton, add 3.2 kms/2 miles +1 hour

❊ = See 'Points of Note' at the end of this walk.

Summary:

*This walk involves a steady climb from
Larkhall to Charlcombe and then a slightly
steeper climb to the MOD offices on
Lansdown. It then proceeds to Langridge on
a fairly level course with a downhill section
at the end. From Langridge to Woolley and
then to Swainswick is more or less level with
a final short climb to Swainswick. The rest is
level or downhill. The route from Bathampton
Meadows to Larkhall in the longer version
crosses the canal, the railway and the River
Avon and is fairly level.*

*Besides four interesting churches in the
four villages, one is also rewarded on a
clear day, with some magnificent views
across the valley towards Bathampton and
further afield to the Westbury White Horse
and wider ranging views of the Wiltshire
Downs and the Mendip Hills.*

*The shorter version omitting Langridge
involves a very steep descent to Woolley.*

Let's Go!

Starting from Bathampton

● Walk down Meadow Lane and just
beyond the canal bridge turn left through a
gate and slightly ahead of you to the left
cross the stone stile onto the towpath.
Follow the towpath to the right for about 1
kilometre until you reach a wooden
footbridge over the canal. At this point look
for a steep flight of steps to your right which
leads to a track that goes under the railway
and then over the river. Turn right into
Grosvenor Bridge Road and follow it to the
left until you reach the main A4 London
Road. Cross the road at the pedestrian
crossing slightly on your right. Turn right and
then first left into Lambridge Street. At the
end of the street cross over St Saviour's
Road to the Larkhall Inn.

Starting from Larkhall

● With the Larkhall Inn on your right, leave St
Saviour's Road behind and take the right fork
in front of you. This is Brookleaze Buildings. At
the first junction, cross the road and then turn
left into Spring Lane keeping the infant school
on your left. Cross at the T-junction (Coxley
Drive/Uphill Drive) and follow the footpath
ahead between the garages and houses.
Ignore the cross-path at 100 metres.

At the end of the row of houses, turn left up
some steps, and then immediately right,
over a culvert, towards a kissing gate
leading into a field with a PRIVATE sign. Bear
left across a field, towards a gap in the
hedge. Then bear diagonally uphill passing
through a gateway and head towards yet
another gateway in the corner of the field.
Proceed towards the top left-hand corner
of the next field (35').

(Walk 12 continues overleaf)

The Holy Well of St Mary at Charlcombe rectory

Emerging onto a road, turn left and take a footpath almost immediately on the right, sloping away from the road. This leads to Charlcombe Church*(2').

● From the church follow the driveway which bears left and joins the road. Turn right and continue up the hill. After passing Manor Farm on your left, look out for a wooden stile on your right about 5m past the driveway for "Hillside" and "Littledown". Cross the stile, and take the path going uphill on your right. Go through several fields always keeping the hedge on your right. Half way up you have to cross a wooden stile.

When you reach the top of this steep section take a much-needed rest and look back on the wide-ranging views (30').

Cross the stone stile and turn right along the edge of the Government buildings to a lane. Turn left and at the next junction turn right. Your path turns left just before an archway. Pass through the smaller of two iron gates and walk along the side of the track as far as a cattle grid. The footpath now follows the right-hand edge of the field on your left until you reach some wooden steps over a wall. Note Beckford Tower, to be seen on the left (10').

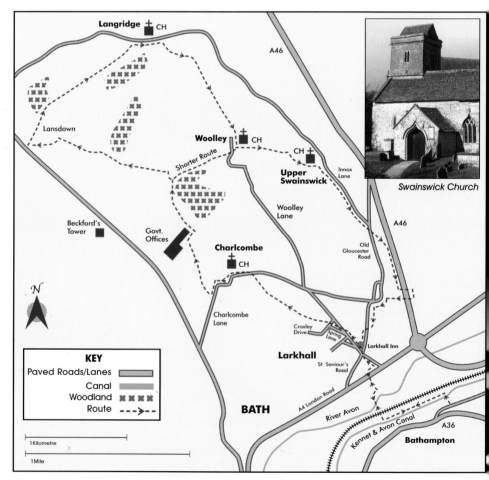

Swainswick Church

KEY

Paved Roads/Lanes
Canal
Woodland
Route

1 Kilometre

1 Mile

42

Walk omitting Langridge

Cross the wall and take the right path to a kissing gate. Go down some steps and down the field to a stile, then a steep track through some woods. After another stile the path goes down diagonally through a field to a gate at the lower left hand corner. Just before the gate the path joins a track. Turn right on to this track, left when the track meets the road and immediately right again along Church Street to see Woolley Church ∗.*

Walk including Langridge

● Cross the wall and take the left path across the field, aiming for a stone stile ahead about 100m from the left-hand corner of the field, in the general direction of a distant communication mast. Go over the stile. Continue in the direction of the mast through the next field to another stile, and keep in a straight line to a wooden gate.

Woolley Church

Go through two more gates 100m apart and continue along the path onto a track. Turn right onto the track and after 50m take the path on your left which goes through a wooden gate into a field (15′).

Cross two fields keeping the wall on your right. Follow the wall as it bears left at the end of the second field and then look for a stone stile (15′).

Cross this stile and head diagonally towards the road to the left of the houses, with the white railings of the racecourse visible beyond. At the cattle grid, turn sharp right down the private driveway. Leave the drive as it bends to the right and cross a stone stile in the wall on your left. Cross this field heading in a 2 o'clock direction and aim for the gate in the bottom right-hand corner of the field. Go through the gate and continue downhill following the fence on your left. As the fence starts to loop away to the left, continue straight on down towards a field bridge over a stream. Cross the bridge, turn immediately left through the gate and cross the stream again using the stepping stones (15′).

● Bear right up the field. At its brow, you will see a stone barn 100m to your left. Carry on to the wooden stile in the hedge. Go straight across the next field towards a house and through a gate. Turn right down the lane. St Mary Magdalene's Church, Langridge ∗, is on your left (10′).

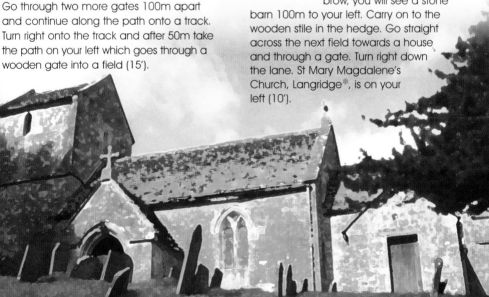
Langridge Church

Continue down the lane until you reach a footpath on the right just before some cottages. Take this path and after 25m, cross the bridge on the left and go straight up the hill, making for a post on the ridge ahead. Bear left along the ridge to a stile and then across the field aiming for another stile straight ahead.

● Bear slightly left across the next field towards a stile next to a gate in the hedge ahead. Continue straight ahead to another stile and then through a gate. Keep the hedge to the right and follow the path to a lane where you turn right into Woolley. After passing a few cottages turn left into Church Street, leading to All Saints Church* (30').

Where the longer and shorter routes join

Take the footpath to the right of the church and continue down a field keeping the hedge on the left. A PF sign points towards the bottom right-hand corner of the field. Cross the Lam Brook at this point and follow the stream around to the right. Cross another small stream and head uphill, following the footpath sign. Head for the house at the left end of a group ahead. The path at this point goes up steps and through the garden of this house onto a lane opposite Swainswick Church* (20').

● Turn right along this lane until you reach the old A46 Gloucester Road. Cross the road and take the private road/footpath to the right. Continue straight ahead until you reach a point where the path turns left over a bridge to cross the A46. Turn right immediately after the crossing and then right again into Bailbrook Lane. This leads to the Gloucester Road again, where you turn left and cross the road. Take the next right turn which takes you through Swainswick Gardens to a path leading to a bridge over Lam Brook. Turn left into St Saviour's Road and go along it to the starting point (45').

Returning to Bathampton

To return to Meadow Lane, turn left from St Saviour's Road into Upper Lambridge Street.

When you reach the main London Road again, turn right, and cross by the pedestrian crossing. Follow Grosvenor Bridge Road round to the right and then left over Grosvenor bridge. Before you reach the railway, take the footpath on your left which continues roughly parallel to the railway line through a couple of fields. Make for the gate on the right-hand corner of the second field. Go through the gate up the track and turn right into Meadow Lane.

POINTS OF NOTE

Charlcombe Church
The Parish Church of St Mary the Virgin has a Norman doorway and font. The Holy Well of St Mary's is in the Rectory Gardens on your left. The villagers used to take the water which was reputed to be good for the eyes.

Langridge Church
The Church is mainly 12th Century Norman with later additions. Two interesting features inside are the Norman chancel arch with three orders of zigzag and, in a round headed recess above, a sculpture of Madonna and Child – probably 13th century. On the southeast corner of the nave outside is a pre-Reformation sundial.

Woolley Church
All Saints Church is of 18th Century Georgian design. It has a plaque to give thanks for the safe return of the men from the parish who served in the First and Second World Wars. Remarkably, they all survived.

Swainswick Church
St Mary's Church Swainswick is 600 years old and has a Norman doorway. Both John Wood the Elder and his son, John Wood the Younger, are buried here.